THE GRAPHIC NOVEL
William Shakespeare

Script by John McDonald

Adapted by Brigit Viney

HEINLE
CENGAGE Learning™

Australia • Brazil • Japan • Korea • Mexico • Singapore • Spain • United Kingdom • United States

HEINLE
CENGAGE Learning™

Macbeth: The Graphic Novel
William Shakespeare
Script by John McDonald
Adapted by Brigit Viney

Publisher: Sherrise Roehr

Editor in Chief: Clive Bryant

Development Editors: John Hicks
   and Jennifer Nunan

Contributing Writer: Amanda Cole

Director of U.S. Marketing:
   Jim McDonough

Content Project Manager: Natalie Griffith

Senior Print Buyer: Mary Beth Hennebury

Cover / Text Designer: Jo Wheeler

Compositor: Jo Wheeler and
   Macmillan Publishing Solutions

Character Designs & Original Artwork:
   Jon Haward

Inking Assistant: Gary Erskine

Coloring & Lettering: Nigel Dobbyn

Audio: EFS Television Production Ltd.

For permission to use material from this text or product, submit all requests online at **cengage.com/permissions**

Further permissions questions can be emailed to **permissionrequest@cengage.com**

ISBN-13: 978-1-4240-2873-3
ISBN-10: 1-4240-2873-6

Heinle
25 Thomson Place
Boston, Massachusetts 02210
USA

Cengage Learning is a leading provider of customized learning solutions with office locations around the globe, including Singapore, the United Kingdom, Australia, Mexico, Brazil and Japan. Locate our local office at: **international.cengage.com/region**

Cengage Learning products are represented in Canada by Nelson Education, Ltd.

Visit Heinle online at **http://elt.heinle.com**
Visit our corporate website at **www.cengage.com**

Published in association with Classical Comics Ltd.

Images on pages 3 & 6 reproduced with the kind permission of the Trustees of the National Library of Scotland. © National Library of Scotland.

Printed in Canada
1 2 3 4 5 6 7 8 9 10 11 10 09

Contents

Characters...4
Introduction...6

Macbeth

Act 1
Act 1 Scene 1 8
Act 1 Scene 2 9
Act 1 Scene 3 12
Act 1 Scene 4 19
Act 1 Scene 5 20
Act 1 Scene 6 23
Act 1 Scene 7 24

Act 2
Act 2 Scene 1 29
Act 2 Scene 2 33
Act 2 Scene 3 38
Act 2 Scene 4 46

Act 3
Act 3 Scene 1 49
Act 3 Scene 2 56
Act 3 Scene 3 59
Act 3 Scene 4 62
Act 3 Scene 5 73
Act 3 Scene 6 76

Act 4
Act 4 Scene 1 78
Act 4 Scene 2 88
Act 4 Scene 3 94

Act 5
Act 5 Scene 1 104
Act 5 Scene 2 108
Act 5 Scene 3 110
Act 5 Scene 4 115
Act 5 Scene 5 117
Act 5 Scene 6 120
Act 5 Scene 7 121
Act 5 Scene 8 124

Glossary...130–132
William Shakespeare 133
The Real Macbeth......................................134
The Real Macbeth Family Tree 135
Summary of the Main Characters
   in Shakespeare's *Macbeth*...............136–137
Link Map of Characters in
   Shakespeare's *Macbeth*............................138
Famous Quotations..........................139–140
Notes 141–143

Characters

Duncan
King of Scotland

Malcolm
Son of Duncan

Donalbain
Son of Duncan

Macduff
*Scottish **Nobleman***

Lenox
*Scottish **Nobleman***

Rosse
*Scottish **Nobleman***

Lady Macbeth
Wife of Macbeth

Lady Macduff
Wife of Macduff

Siward
*Leader of the English **Army***

A lady who ***serves***
Lady Macbeth

Seyton
*A man who **serves** Macbeth*

An English Doctor

A Scottish Doctor

A **Porter**

An Old Man

First Murderer

Second Murderer

Third Murderer

Characters

Macbeth
A leader in the King's **Army**

Banquo
A leader in the King's **Army**

The Ghost of Banquo

Menteth
Scottish **Nobleman**

Angus
Scottish **Nobleman**

Cathness
Scottish **Nobleman**

Young Siward
Son of Siward

Fleance
Son of Banquo

Boy
Son of Macduff

First **Witch**

Second **Witch**

Third **Witch**

Hecate
The "Queen" **Witch**

and **Lords**, Ladies,
Officers, Soldiers,
Messengers, Ghosts,
and **Spirits**.

Introduction

It is Scotland in the year 1040.

King Duncan has **ruled** the land for six years, since the death of his grandfather. He is a good king, but Scotland is not a peaceful country. It has been divided in two for centuries. **Vikings** live in the north, and **Saxons** live in the south. Each small group of **Vikings** or **Saxons** has its own strong leader who is a great fighter.

Now that Duncan is king, all the different groups have a chance to come together and form a single nation. However some leaders do not welcome this. They want to remain independent, and they continue to fight against Duncan. Sometimes they are joined by groups of fighters from Ireland and Norway. Some of them would even like to be King of Scotland themselves.

Duncan sends a powerful **army** to fight against these groups who do not accept him as king. The **army** is led by a number of **noblemen** who are experienced soldiers. The greatest and most trusted of these is King Duncan's **cousin.** This is the **Thane** of Glamis, whose name is …

… Macbeth.

Macbeth

A Scottish heath ...

WHERE HAVE YOU BEEN, SISTER?

KILLING PIGS.

WHAT ABOUT YOU, SISTER?

A SAILOR'S WIFE WAS EATING NUTS. "GIVE ME SOME," I SAID.

"GO AWAY, WITCH!" SHE SHOUTED.

HER HUSBAND'S SAILED TO ALEPPO. I'M GOING TO MAKE HIS LIFE TERRIBLE ON THE SHIP.

I'LL GIVE YOU A WIND.

YOU'RE KIND.

I'LL GIVE YOU ONE, TOO.

15

AND *THANE* OF CAWDOR.

THAT'S WHAT THEY SAID!

WHO'S THIS?

THE KING IS *DELIGHTED* WITH THE NEWS OF YOUR SUCCESS, MACBETH.

HE HAS SENT US TO TAKE YOU TO HIM.

HE'S DECIDED TO MAKE YOU *THANE* OF CAWDOR.

WHAT! CAN THE *DEVIL* SPEAK THE TRUTH?

BUT THE *THANE* OF CAWDOR IS STILL ALIVE.

HE WILL DIE SOON BECAUSE HE FOUGHT AGAINST THE KING.

GLAMIS AND CAWDOR. THE GREATEST WILL FOLLOW.

THANK YOU.

The King's *palace* at Forres. King Duncan is waiting for Macbeth and Banquo ...

IS CAWDOR DEAD?

YES, MY *LORD*. THEY SAY THAT HE ASKED FOR *YOUR HIGHNESS'S FORGIVENESS* AND THAT HE WAS DEEPLY SORRY.

HE DIED VERY *BRAVELY*.

I TRUSTED HIM SO MUCH.

MY DEAR *COUSIN!* I CAN NEVER REPAY YOU FOR WHAT YOU'VE DONE!

I WAS JUST DOING MY DUTY, *YOUR HIGHNESS*.

I'LL MAKE SURE YOU BECOME A GREAT MAN.

AND YOU, TOO, BANQUO.

I ONLY WANT TO *SERVE* YOU, MY LORD.

I HAVE SOMETHING TO TELL EVERYONE.

I'VE CHOSEN MY ELDEST SON, MALCOLM, TO BE KING AFTER ME. FROM NOW ON, HIS *TITLE* WILL BE THE PRINCE OF CUMBERLAND.

19

NOW, LET'S GO TO INVERNESS AND VISIT YOUR CASTLE.

I'LL GO ON AHEAD TO TELL MY WIFE.

WHAT A GOOD MAN YOU ARE, CAWDOR!

MALCOLM! HE'S IN MY WAY NOW. I DON'T WANT TO THINK ABOUT WHAT I MIGHT DO ...

LET'S QUICKLY FOLLOW MACBETH TO HIS CASTLE.

Act One
Scene Five

At Macbeth's castle in Inverness, Lady Macbeth receives news from her husband ...

"THREE *WITCHES* TOLD ME I WOULD BE *THANE* OF CAWDOR. THEN I WAS MADE *THANE* OF CAWDOR."

"THEY ALSO TOLD ME I WOULD BE KING! I HAD TO TELL YOU IMMEDIATELY, MY DEAREST."

YOU'RE *THANE* OF GLAMIS AND CAWDOR! AND YOU WILL BE KING! BUT YOU'RE TOO KIND TO DO WHAT YOU HAVE TO DO TO BECOME KING.

WHAT YOU WANT ISN'T YOURS. TO GET IT, YOU'LL HAVE TO DO SOMETHING THAT YOU'RE AFRAID TO DO.

HURRY HOME. I'LL MAKE SURE NOTHING GETS IN THE WAY OF OUR GOLDEN FUTURE.

THANE OF GLAMIS! AND THANE OF CAWDOR! YOUR LETTER HAS MADE ME SO HAPPY.

DUNCAN'S COMING HERE TONIGHT, MY LOVE.

AND WHEN IS HE LEAVING?

TOMORROW.

HE'LL NEVER SEE TOMORROW! YOU MUSTN'T LET PEOPLE KNOW WHAT YOU'RE PLANNING. YOU MUST WELCOME HIM PROPERLY ...

... AND GIVE HIM DINNER. LEAVE THE REAL BUSINESS OF THE NIGHT TO ME.

WE'LL TALK LATER.

JUST BE CLEAR IN YOUR MIND. LEAVE THE REST TO ME.

After the meal, Banquo and his son cannot rest ...

WHAT TIME IS IT, SON?

I DON'T KNOW, BUT THE MOON'S GONE DOWN.

IT'S ABOUT TWELVE, THEN.

I THINK IT'S LATER, FATHER.

WAIT. TAKE MY SWORD. HERE, TAKE THIS, TOO.

I'M TIRED, BUT I CAN'T SLEEP BECAUSE OF THE TERRIBLE DREAMS I HAVE.

WHO'S THERE?

A FRIEND.

AREN'T YOU IN BED YET? THE KING'S IN BED. HE HAD A WONDERFUL TIME.

HE'S GIVEN THIS DIAMOND TO YOUR WIFE TO THANK HER FOR THE EVENING.

WE DIDN'T HAVE TIME TO PREPARE WELL FOR HIM.

29

THERE IS NO *DAGGER!* THE THOUGHT OF MURDER IS MAKING ME IMAGINE IT. *WITCHES* ARE OUT, AND MURDER IS WALKING AROUND SILENTLY LIKE A GHOST.

DONG! DONG!

SOLID EARTH. I NEED SILENCE FOR WHAT I'M GOING TO DO.

THAT'S ENOUGH TALK. TOO MUCH TALKING STOPS US FROM DOING WHAT WE HAVE TO DO.

THE *BELL'S* CALLING ME. DON'T HEAR IT, DUNCAN. IT'S CALLING YOU TO *HEAVEN* OR TO *HELL.*

32

Later ...

THE WINE THAT MADE THEM DRUNK HAS MADE ME *BRAVE.* MACBETH'S MURDERING THE KING RIGHT NOW.

WHO'S THERE? WHO IS IT?

OH NO! THEY'VE WOKEN UP! I LEFT THEIR *DAGGERS* READY FOR HIM. THEY WERE EASY FOR HIM TO SEE.

MY HUSBAND!

I'VE DONE IT.

33

35

AND DRINK CAN MAKE YOU SLEEP, SIR.

AND IT DID THIS TO YOU LAST NIGHT?

IT DID, SIR.

IS YOUR *MASTER* UP?

HERE HE COMES.

GOOD MORNING, SIR!

GOOD MORNING TO YOU BOTH!

IS THE KING UP?

NOT YET.

HE TOLD ME TO CALL EARLY.

41

43

Act Three
Scene One

Macbeth is now King of Scotland.
In the King's *palace* at Forres, Banquo thinks Macbeth has done something wrong ...

TRUMPET!

TRUMPET!

HERE'S OUR MOST IMPORTANT GUEST.

OUR CELEBRATION WOULDN'T BE COMPLETE WITHOUT HIM.

YOU HAVE IT ALL NOW AS THE *WITCHES* PROMISED. I THINK YOU HAVE DONE SOMETHING TERRIBLE TO GET IT.

BUT IF THEY WERE RIGHT ABOUT YOU, THEN THEY MIGHT BE RIGHT ABOUT ME.

WE'RE HAVING A GREAT DINNER TONIGHT, AND WE'D LIKE YOU TO BE THERE.

OF COURSE.

49

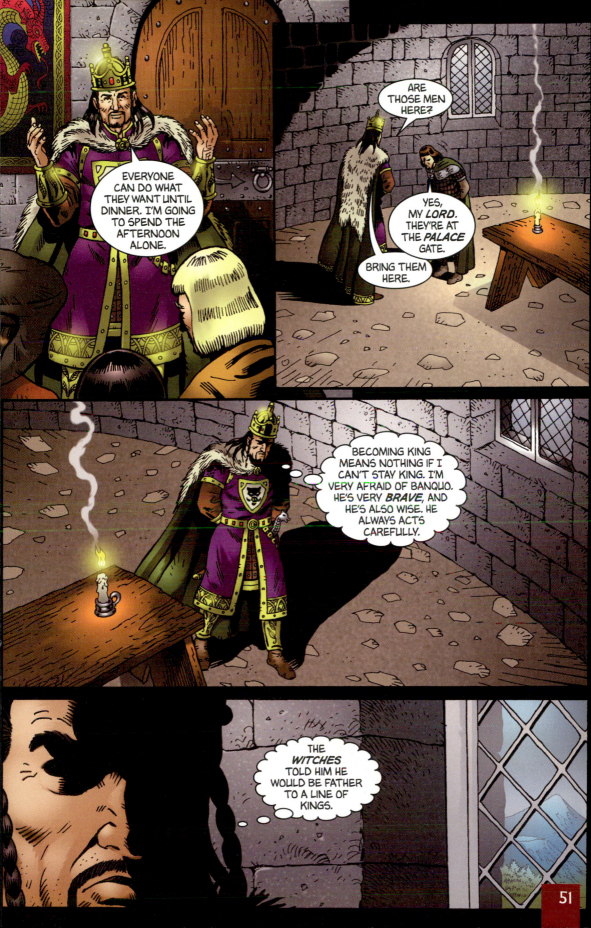

EVERYONE CAN DO WHAT THEY WANT UNTIL DINNER. I'M GOING TO SPEND THE AFTERNOON ALONE.

ARE THOSE MEN HERE?

YES, MY *LORD*. THEY'RE AT THE *PALACE* GATE.

BRING THEM HERE.

BECOMING KING MEANS NOTHING IF I CAN'T STAY KING. I'M VERY AFRAID OF BANQUO. HE'S VERY *BRAVE*, AND HE'S ALSO WISE. HE ALWAYS ACTS CAREFULLY.

THE *WITCHES* TOLD HIM HE WOULD BE FATHER TO A LINE OF KINGS.

IF THAT'S TRUE, THEN HIS FAMILY WILL TAKE EVERYTHING AWAY FROM ME.

BANG!

I'VE MURDERED DUNCAN FOR BANQUO'S FAMILY! I'VE LOST MY PEACE OF MIND AND SOLD MYSELF TO THE *DEVIL* TO MAKE THEM KINGS! I CAN'T LET THAT HAPPEN.

WHO'S THERE!

WAIT OUTSIDE THE DOOR.

WAS IT YESTERDAY WE SPOKE?

IT WAS, *YOUR HIGHNESS.*

I'LL TELL YOU WHERE TO WAIT FOR HIM. YOU HAVE TO DO IT TONIGHT AND NOT NEAR THE *PALACE*.

HIS SON WILL BE WITH HIM, AND HE MUST DIE, TOO.

GO AND PREPARE YOURSELVES. I'LL COME TO YOU SOON.

WE ARE PREPARED, MY *LORD*.

THEN STAY IN THE CASTLE. I'LL CALL YOU SOON.

IT'S ARRANGED. BANQUO, YOU WILL FIND OUT TONIGHT IF YOU'RE GOING TO *HEAVEN*.

57

WHAT HAPPENED TO THE LIGHT?

WASN'T THAT THE PLAN?

ONLY ONE OF THEM IS DEAD. THE SON HAS ESCAPED.

WE'VE ONLY DONE HALF THE JOB.

WELL, LET'S GO AND TELL MACBETH WHAT WE HAVE DONE.

GOOD NIGHT! GOOD NIGHT!

I WILL BE PUNISHED. BLOOD WILL HAVE BLOOD, THEY SAY.

MACDUFF REFUSED TO COME TO THE DINNER.

WHY?

WHAT TIME IS IT?

IT'S ALMOST MORNING.

I DON'T KNOW, BUT I'LL FIND OUT. SOMEONE IN HIS HOUSE WILL TELL ME.

TOMORROW I'LL GO AND FIND THE *WITCHES*.

I MUST MAKE SURE I'M SAFE. I'VE GOT SO MUCH BLOOD ON MY HANDS THAT I CAN'T TURN BACK NOW. THERE ARE SOME THINGS I MUST DO SOON, BEFORE I THINK TOO MUCH ABOUT THEM.

YOU NEED TO SLEEP.

YES. LET'S GO TO BED.

87

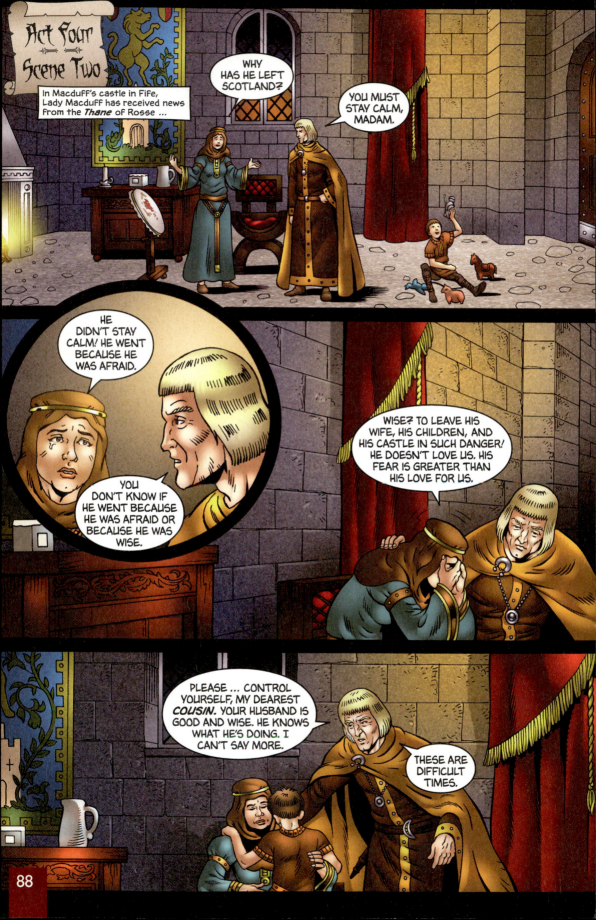

WHAT ILLNESS DOES HE MEAN?

IT'S CALLED "THE *EVIL.*" THE KING MAKES IT GO AWAY WHEN HE PRAYS OVER THE PERSON.

HE CAN ALSO SEE WHAT WILL HAPPEN IN THE FUTURE. GOD HAS GIVEN HIM SOME VERY SPECIAL GIFTS.

WHO'S THIS?

I DON'T KNOW.

IT'S MY *COUSIN!*

AH, WELCOME, ROSSE!

THANK YOU, SIR.

ARE THINGS STILL THE SAME IN SCOTLAND?

99

THEY'RE TERRIBLE. THERE IS SO MUCH KILLING THAT NOBODY NOTICES IT ANY MORE.

IT'S TRUE.

WHAT IS THE LATEST *HORROR?*

THERE'S A NEW ONE EVERY MINUTE.

HOW ARE MY WIFE AND CHILDREN?

THEY'RE ... WELL.

MACBETH HASN'T ATTACKED THEM?

NO. THEY WERE FINE ... WHEN I LEFT THEM.

TELL ME MORE. HOW ARE THINGS?

Late at night in Dunsinane Castle ...

I'VE BEEN HERE FOR TWO NIGHTS, BUT I'VE SEEN NOTHING. WHEN DID SHE LAST WALK?

SINCE THE KING WENT TO WAR, SHE'S DONE IT. SHE GETS OUT OF BED, UNLOCKS HER CUPBOARD, TAKES OUT SOME PAPER, WRITES ON IT, READS IT, AND THEN GOES BACK TO BED. ALL THE TIME SHE'S ASLEEP.

DOES SHE SAY ANYTHING?

I WON'T REPEAT WHAT SHE SAYS, SIR.

YOU CAN TELL ME. AND YOU SHOULD.

NO, SIR. I WON'T TELL ANYONE.

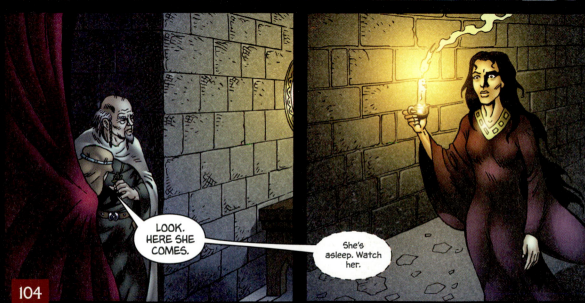

LOOK. HERE SHE COMES.

SHE'S ASLEEP. WATCH HER.

Where did she get that light?

It was by her bed. She insists on having a light near her all the time.

Her eyes are open.

But they don't see anything.

What is she doing with her hands?

She always does that. It's as if she were washing them.

THERE'S STILL SOMETHING THERE.

Listen! She's speaking. I'll write down what she says.

OUT! OUT, I SAY!

SHAME, MY *LORD*, SHAME! A SOLDIER AND AFRAID? NO ONE CAN QUESTION US.

BUT WE DIDN'T KNOW THE OLD MAN HAD SO MUCH BLOOD IN HIM ...

105

WASH YOUR HANDS! DON'T LOOK SO FRIGHTENED.

BANQUO'S DEAD.

Not that, too?

LET'S GO TO BED. SOMEONE'S KNOCKING AT THE GATE.

COME. GIVE ME YOUR HAND.

WILL SHE GO BACK TO BED NOW?

YES.

ALL THESE TERRIBLE EVENTS CAN CAUSE INSANITY LIKE THIS. THEN PEOPLE WITH SICK MINDS TELL THEIR SECRETS TO THEIR PILLOWS.

TAKE CARE OF HER. MAKE SURE SHE CAN'T HURT HERSELF, AND WATCH HER ALL THE TIME. GOOD NIGHT. I WON'T SAY WHAT I'M THINKING.

GOOD NIGHT, DOCTOR.

Act Five
Scene Three

At Dunsinane, Macbeth receives news of Malcolm's *army* ...

DON'T BRING ME ANY MORE REPORTS! I DON'T CARE IF EVERYONE LEAVES ME. NOTHING WILL HURT ME UNTIL BIRNAM WOOD COMES TO DUNSINANE. AND I DON'T CARE ABOUT MALCOLM BECAUSE HE WAS BORN OF A WOMAN.

THE *SPIRIT* TOLD ME, "NOBODY WHO WAS BORN OF A WOMAN WILL HURT YOU."

LEAVE ME AND JOIN THE ENGLISH IF YOU WANT! I WILL NEVER BE AFRAID!

WHAT DO YOU WANT, YOU FOOL? WHY ARE YOU LOOKING LIKE THAT?

THERE ARE TEN THOUSAND ...

BIRDS?

SOLDIERS, SIR.

CAN'T YOU *MEND* A SICK MIND? CAN'T YOU CLEAN AWAY THE TROUBLES OF THE HEART?

ONLY SHE CAN DO THAT.

THEN THROW YOUR MEDICINE TO THE DOGS!

PUT ON MY *ARMOR!*

SEYTON, SEND OUT THE HORSEMEN!

THE *THANES* ARE LEAVING ME.

SEND THEM OUT!

SCREAMS LIKE THAT USED TO MAKE ME FRIGHTENED. BUT I'VE SEEN SO MUCH HORROR RECENTLY THAT NOTHING BOTHERS ME NOW.

Moments later ...

WHAT WAS THAT CRY FOR?

THE QUEEN ... IS DEAD, MY LORD.

HER LIFE HAS ENDED TOO SOON. BUT WHAT DOES IT MATTER?

TOMORROW, AND TOMORROW, AND TOMORROW. EACH DAY SHOWS US THE WAY TO DEATH.

AND NOW HER SMALL CANDLE IS OUT.

LIFE IS JUST A WALKING SHADOW. IT'S A STORY THAT A FOOL TELLS – FULL OF NOISE BUT WITH NO MEANING.

125

I'M SAD THAT WE LOST SOME OF OUR FRIENDS.

SOME HAD TO DIE. WE DIDN'T LOSE MANY.

MACDUFF IS MISSING, AND SO IS YOUR SON.

YOUR SON WAS KILLED, MY *LORD.* BUT HE DIED LIKE A MAN.

HE'S DEAD?

YES. HE WAS BROUGHT OFF THE *BATTLEFIELD.*

WERE HIS INJURIES ON THE FRONT OF HIS BODY?

YES.

Macbeth

End

Glossary

A

admit /æd ˈmɪt/ — (admits, admitting, admitted) If you admit that something bad, unpleasant, or embarrassing is true, you agree, often reluctantly, that it is true. *He rarely admits to making errors.*

armor /ˈar mər/ In former times, armor was special metal clothing that soldiers wore for protection in battle.

army /ˈar mi/ — (armies) An army is a large, organized group of people who are armed and trained to fight on land in a war. Most armies are organized and controlled by governments.

B

bang /bæŋ/ — (bangs) A bang is a sudden, loud noise such as the noise of an explosion.

battle /ˈbæ tᵊl/ — (battles) A battle is a violent fight between groups of people, especially one between military forces during a war.

battlefield /ˈbæ tᵊl fild/ — (battlefields) A battlefield is a place where a battle is fought.

bell /bɛl/ — (bells) A bell is a hollow metal object with a loose piece hanging inside it that hits the sides and makes a sound.

betray /bɪt ˈreɪ/ — (betrays, betraying, betrayed) If someone betrays their country or their friends, they give information to an enemy, putting their country's security or their friends' safety at risk.

brave /breɪv/ — (braver, bravest) Someone who is brave is willing to do things that are dangerous and does not show fear in difficult or dangerous situations. *She became an extremely brave horsewoman.*

bubble /ˈbʌ bᵊl/ — (bubbles, bubbling, bubbled) When a liquid bubbles, bubbles move in it, for example, because it is boiling or moving quickly.

C

cave /keɪv/ — (caves) A cave is a large hole in the side of a cliff or hill or under the ground.

cousin /ˈkʌ zᵊn/ — (cousins) Your cousin is the child of your uncle or aunt.

coward /ˈkaʊ ərd/ — (cowards) A coward is someone who is easily frightened and avoids dangerous or difficult situations.

crack /kræk/ — (cracks) A crack is a sharp sound, like the sound of a piece of wood breaking.

crash /kræʃ/ — (crashes) A crash is a sudden, loud noise. *Two people recalled hearing a loud crash about 1:30 am.*

curse /kɜs/ — (curses, cursing, cursed) If you curse someone or something, you say impolite or insulting things about them because you are angry. *We started driving again, cursing the delay.*

D

dagger /ˈdæ gər/ — (daggers) A dagger is a weapon like a knife with two sharp edges.

delighted /dɪ ˈlaɪtɪd/ If you are delighted, you are extremely pleased and excited about something. *Frank was delighted to see her.* Delight is a feeling of very great pleasure.

devil /ˈdɛ vᵊl/ — (devils) A devil is an evil spirit.

diamond /ˈdaɪ mənd/ — (diamonds) A diamond is a hard, bright, precious stone which is clear and colorless. Diamonds are used in jewelry and for cutting very hard substances.

dong /dɔŋ/ — (dongs) A dong is the sound a bell makes.

dragon /ˈdræ gən/ — (dragons) In stories and legends, a dragon is an animal like a big lizard. It has wings and claws and breathes out fire.

drum /drʌm/ — (drums) A drum is a musical instrument consisting of a skin stretched tightly over a round frame.

E

enemy /ˈɛ nə mi/ — (enemies) If someone is your enemy, they hate you or want to harm you.

evil /ˈi vᵊl/ Evil is used to refer to all the wicked and bad things that happen in the world. *... the battle between good and evil*

F

flag /flæg/ — (flags) A flag is a piece of colored cloth used as a sign for something or as a signal. *... the Spanish flag*

forgiveness /fər ˈgɪv nɪs/ Forgiveness is the act of forgiving. If you forgive someone who has done something wrong, you stop being angry with them and no longer want to punish them. *He fell to his knees and begged for forgiveness.*

G

gather /'gæ ðər/ — (gathers, gathering, gathered) If people gather somewhere or if someone gathers them, they come together in a group. *We gathered around the fireplace.*

gentleman /'dʒɛn tᵊl mən/ — (gentlemen) You can refer politely to men as gentlemen. *This way, please, gentlemen.*

greedy /'gri di/ — (greedier, greediest) If you describe someone as greedy, you mean that they want to have more of something such as food or money than is necessary or fair.

H

hail /heɪl/ — (hails, hailing, hailed) If a person, event, or achievement is hailed as important or successful, they are praised publicly. *US magazines hailed her as the greatest rock 'n' roll singer in the world.*

health /hɛlθ/ Health is a state in which a person is fit and well. *In the hospital they nursed me back to health.*

heaven /'hɛ vən/ — (heavens) In some religions, heaven is said to be the place where God lives and where good people go when they die.

hedgehog /'hedʒ hɔg/ — (hedgehogs) A hedgehog is a small brown animal with sharp spikes covering its back.

hell /hel/ In some religions, hell is the place where the Devil lives and where bad people are sent when they die.

horrible /'hɔ rɪ bᵊl/ If you describe something or someone as horrible, you mean that they are very unpleasant.

horror /'hɔ rər/ Horror is a feeling of great shock, fear, and worry caused by something extremely unpleasant. *I felt numb with horror.*

hostess /'hoʊ stɪs/ — (hostesses) The hostess at a party is the woman who has invited the guests and provides the food, drink, or entertainment.

L

lord /lɔrd/ — (lords) A lord is a man who has a high rank in the nobility, for example, an earl, a viscount, or a marquis.

M

master /'mæs tər/ — (masters) A servant's master is the man that he or she works for.

mend /mɛnd/ — (mends, mending, mended) If you mend something that is damaged or broken, you repair it so that it works properly or can be used. *They mended the leaking roof.*

messenger /'me sɪn dʒər/ — (messengers) A messenger takes a message or package to someone or takes messages regularly as their job. *The document was sent by messenger.*

N

nobleman /'noʊ bᵊl mən/ — (noblemen) If someone is a nobleman, he belongs to a high social class and has a title.

nut /nʌt/ — (nuts) The firm shelled fruit of some trees and bushes are called nuts.

P

palace /'pæ lɪs/ — (palaces) A palace is a very large impressive house, especially the home of a king, queen, or president.

porter /'pɔr tər/ — (porters) A porter is a person whose job is to carry things, for example, people's luggage at a train station or in a hotel.

pour /pɔr/ — (pours, pouring, poured) If you pour a liquid or other substance, you make it flow steadily out of a container by holding the container at an angle. *She poured some water into a plastic bowl.*

R

revenge /rɪ 'vɛndʒ/ Revenge involves hurting or punishing someone who has hurt or harmed you. *The other children took revenge on the boy, claiming he was a school bully.*

rule /rul/ — (rules, ruling, ruled) The person or group that rules a country controls its affairs. *Emperor Hirohito ruled Japan for 62 years until his death in 1989.*

S

Saxon /'sæk sən/ — (Saxons) A Saxon is a person belonging to the Germanic people that conquered parts of England in the 5th to 6th century.

scream /skrim/ — (screams, screaming, screamed) When someone screams, they make a very loud, high-pitched cry, for example, because they are in pain or are very frightened. *He screamed, screaming in agony.*

servant /ˈsɜr vᵊnt/ — (servants) A servant is someone who is employed to work at another person's home, for example, as a cleaner or a gardener.

serve /sɜrv/ — (serves, serving, served) If you serve your country, an organization, or a person, you do useful work for them. *He served the government loyally for 30 years.*

smash /smæʃ/ — (smashes, smashing, smashed) If you smash something or if it smashes, it breaks into many pieces, for example, when it is hit or dropped. *Two or three glasses fell and smashed into pieces.*

spirit /ˈspɪ rɪt/ — (spirits) A person's spirit is the non-physical part of the person that is believed to remain alive after their death. A spirit is a ghost or supernatural being.

stupid /ˈstu pɪd/ — (stupider, stupidest) If you say that someone or something is stupid, you mean that they show a lack of good judgment or intelligence and they are not at all sensible. *I made a stupid mistake.*

surrender /sə ˈrɛn dər/ — (surrenders, surrendering, surrendered) If you surrender, you stop fighting or resisting someone and agree that you have been beaten. *He surrendered to American troops. / . . . after the Japanese surrender in 1945*

sword /sɔrd/ — (swords) A sword is a weapon with a handle and a long, sharp blade.

thane /θeɪn/ — (thanes) A thane is a man ranking between ordinary freemen and nobles and is granted land by the king or by lords for military service.

thud /θʌd/ — (thuds, thudding, thudded) A thud is a dull sound, such as that which a heavy object makes when it hits something soft.

title /ˈtaɪ tᵊl/ — (titles) Someone's title is a word such as "Doctor," "Mr.," or "Mrs." that is used before their own name in order to show their status or profession.

toad /toʊd/ — (toads) A toad is an animal like a frog, but with drier skin.

toil /tɔɪl/ — (toils, toiling, toiled) When people toil, they work very hard doing unpleasant or tiring tasks. *Workers toiled long hours.*

traitor /ˈtreɪ tər/ — (traitors) A traitor is someone who betrays their country, friends, or a group of which they are a member by helping its enemies.

trumpet /ˈtrʌm pɪt/ — (trumpets) A trumpet is a brass musical instrument.

U

uncle /ˈʌŋ kᵊl/ — (uncles) Your uncle is the brother of your mother or father or the husband of your aunt.

Viking /ˈvaɪkɪŋ/ — (Vikings) A Viking is any of the Scandinavian sea pirates who raided and settled in parts of northwestern Europe in the 8th to 11th century.

W

weapon /ˈwɛ pən/ — (weapons) A weapon is an object such as a gun, a knife, or a missile which is used to kill or hurt people in a fight or a war.

witch /wɪtʃ/ — (witches) In fairy tales, a witch is a woman, usually an old woman, who has evil magic powers.

Your Highness /yɔr ˈhaɪ nɪs/ — (Highnesses) You use expressions such as Your Highness and His Highness to address or refer to a member of a royal family.

William Shakespeare

(c. 1564 - 1616 AD)

Many people believe that William Shakespeare was the greatest writer in the English language. He wrote 38 plays, 154 sonnets, and five poems. His plays have been translated into every major living language.

The actual date of Shakespeare's birth is unknown. Most people accept that his birth date was April 23, 1564. He died 52 years later on the same date.

The life of William Shakespeare can be divided into three acts. He lived in the small village of Stratford-upon-Avon until he was 20 years old. There, he studied, got married, and had children. Then Shakespeare lived as an actor and playwright (a writer of plays) in London. Finally, when he was about 50, Shakespeare retired back to his hometown. He enjoyed some wealth gained from his successful years of work but died a few years later.

William Shakespeare was the oldest son of tradesman John Shakespeare and Mary Arden. He was the third of eight children. William Shakespeare was lucky to survive childhood. Sixteenth century England was filled with diseases such as smallpox, tuberculosis, typhus, and dysentery. Most people did not live longer than 35 years. Three of Shakespeare's seven siblings died from what was probably the Bubonic Plague.

Few records exist about Shakespeare's life. According to most accounts, he went to the local grammar school and studied English literature and Latin. When he was 18 years old, he married Anne Hathaway. She was a local farmer's daughter. They had three children: Susanna in 1583, and twins Hamnet and Judith in 1585. Hamnet, Shakespeare's only son, died when he was 11.

Shakespeare moved to London in 1587. He was an actor at The Globe Theatre. This was one of the largest theaters in England. He appeared in public as a poet in 1593. Later on, in 1599, he became part-owner of The Globe.

When Queen Elizabeth died in 1603, her cousin James became King. He supported Shakespeare and his actors. He allowed them to be called the "King's Men" as long as they entertained the court.

During 1590 and 1613, Shakespeare wrote his plays, sonnets, and poems. The first plays are thought to have been comedies and histories. He was to become famous for both types of writing. Next, he mainly wrote tragedies until about 1608. These included *Hamlet, King Lear,* and *Macbeth,* which are considered three of the best examples of writing in the English language. In his last phase, Shakespeare wrote tragicomedies, also known as romances. His final play was *Henry VII,* written two years before his death.

The cause of Shakespeare's death is unknown. He was buried at the Church of the Holy Trinity in Stratford-upon-Avon. His gravestone has the words (believed to have been written by Shakespeare himself) on it:

Good friend for Jesus' sake forbear
To dig the dust enclosed here!
Blessed be the man that spares these stones,
And cursed be he that moves my bones.

In his will, Shakespeare left most of his possessions to his oldest daughter, Susanna. He left his wife, Anne, his "second best bed." Nobody knows what this gift meant. Shakespeare's last direct descendant, his granddaughter, died in 1670.

The Real Macbeth

(c. 1005 - 1057 AD)

Macbeth is one of Shakespeare's most famous characters. Yet many people don't know that the story is based on historical events. It is thought that Shakespeare read early historical books which tell the history of England, Scotland, and Ireland. However, he changed these historical events considerably to make his play more entertaining for us, his audience.

Although it is impossible to know all the facts, according to history Mac Bethad (Macbeth) was King of Scotland from 1040 to 1057. The name "Mac Bethad" means "son of life." It is actually an Irish name, not a Scottish name.

Scotland in the eleventh century was a cruel place to live. It had many wars, and mass killings occurred often. Whoever ruled Scotland had to protect his family, his community, and the land from his **enemies**. However, many of a ruler's **enemies** were actually the people closest to him. These **enemies** were usually unhappy and jealous relatives who wanted to be king themselves.

Enemies of the king would form a group and challenge the ruler. This happened because a king could choose the next king. In other words, kings didn't simply pass the rule straight onto their oldest sons or closest relative. In Mac Bethad's time, the king could choose who he wanted to replace him. Many people were murdered by their jealous relatives.

Mac Bethad was born around 1005. He was the son of Findláech mac Ruaidrí who was a High Steward in the north of Scotland. It is thought that Mac Bethad's mother was Donada, the second child of King Malcolm II. This means that Mac Bethad was the grandson of a king.

In 1020, Mac Bethad's father died. It is thought that he was murdered by his brother's son. Mac Bethad's **cousin** became High Steward. Twelve years later, Mac Bethad's cousin was killed as punishment for murdering Mac Bethad's father, and Mac Bethad became High Steward.

Mac Bethad then married his **cousin's** widow, Gruoch (Lady Macbeth). She had one son, named Lulach. Gruoch was the granddaughter of Kenneth III. Their marriage meant that Mac Bethad had a very good claim to the Scottish throne.

However Donnchad mac Crínáin (King Duncan I) was the king already. Although Donnchad mac Crínáin should have made friends with his unhappy relatives, including Mac Bethad, he didn't. This was a mistake. It meant that Mac Bethad finally killed Donnchad mac Crínáin in 1040. One historical tale says that Mac Bethad and Banquo cleverly sent the king a sleeping potion and killed him while he was asleep. Mac Bethad became king.

History states that Mac Bethad was a very good king. His kingdom became more stable and wealthier. Mac Bethad even traveled overseas while he was king, which shows how much confidence he had during his rule.

In 1054, Donnchad's son, Máel Coluim mac Donnchad (Malcolm), opposed Mac Bethad's rule. Máel Coluim and his supporters took control of southern Scotland. Three years later, in 1057, Mac Bethad's **army** finally lost against Máel Coluim's **army**. Mac Bethad was killed in battle. It is thought that he was buried in the graveyard at Saint Oran's Chapel on the Isle of Iona. He is the last of many kings to be buried there.

No one knows what happened to Mac Bethad's wife, Gruoch. In Shakespeare's play, she goes insane and dies, although there is no historical account of what actually happened to her.

Unlike in Shakespeare's play, Mac Bethad's death did not mean that Duncan's son became king. First, Gruoch's son, Lulach, became the Scottish ruler. However, Lulach was a weak king. His people laughed at him for being foolish. He was quickly murdered — and that's when Máel Coluim became king.

The Real Macbeth Family Tree

Key:
Parent of ———
Married ≡≡≡

"Malcolm I"
King 943-954
Máel Coluim mac Domnaill

"Duff"
King 962-966
Duib mac Máel Coluim

"Kenneth II"
King 971-995
Cináeda mac Máel Coluim

Domnall

"Kenneth III"
King 997-1005
Cináeda mac Duib

"Malcolm II"
King 1005-1034
Máel Coluim mac Cináeda

Ruadri

First wife (name unknown) — 1 — Boite mac Cináeda — 2 — Gruoch

Máel Brigté

Mormaer of Moray
Findláech mac Ruaidrí

Donada

Bethoc (oldest)

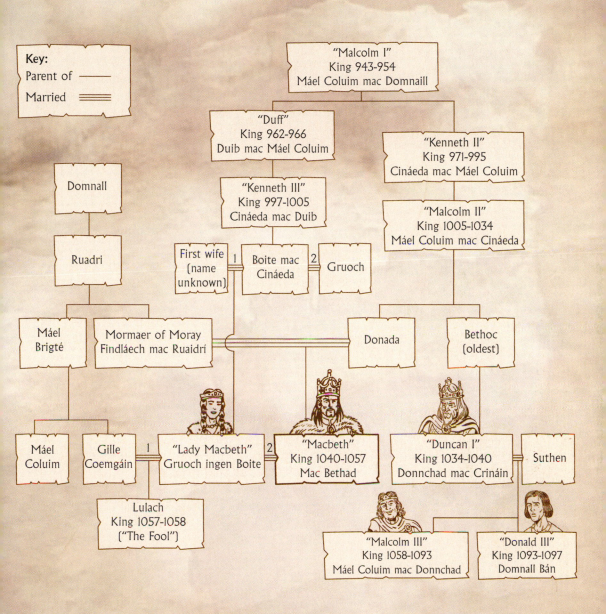

Máel Coluim

Gille Coemgáin — 1 — "Lady Macbeth" Gruoch ingen Boite — 2 — "Macbeth" King 1040-1057 Mac Bethad

"Duncan I"
King 1034-1040
Donnchad mac Crináin

Suthen

Lulach
King 1057-1058
("The Fool")

"Malcolm III"
King 1058-1093
Máel Coluim mac Donnchad

"Donald III"
King 1093-1097
Domnall Bán

Summary of the Main Characters in Shakespeare's Macbeth

Macbeth, *Thane* of Glamis

Macbeth is a leader in the king's **army,** but he is not satisfied with this, and his greed makes him want even more success. He becomes the **Thane** of Cawdor after defeating the **Vikings.** The **witches'** predictions and his wife's encouragement lead him to kill Duncan and become King of Scotland. Although **brave** in **battle,** he is an insecure and unfair ruler.

Lady Macbeth, Macbeth's wife

She wants power and wealth more than anything else, and she encourages Macbeth to murder Duncan. In the end, her guilt makes her crazy, and she suffers nightmares, starts sleepwalking, and becomes obsessed with the blood on her hands which no one else can see.

Duncan, King of Scotland

He is a kind and trusting older king. His kindness allows Macbeth to attack him. Macbeth kills him (and his two guards) with a **dagger.** Duncan's death and his sons' escape means Macbeth is made king.

Malcolm and Donalbain, Duncan's sons

These two men are King Duncan's sons. When their father dies, they flee to avoid being murdered themselves. Donalbain escapes to Ireland. Malcolm goes to England where he hopes to build an **army** to take back the kingdom from the **evil** Macbeth. At the end of the play, after Macbeth is defeated, Malcolm becomes king.

Three *Witches*, the Weird Sisters

The three **witches** have a very important role in this play. They tell Macbeth that he will be **Thane** of Cawdor, **Thane** of Glamis, and eventually King. Their predictions lead Macbeth to commit many murders. At the same time, however, they predict that while Banquo may not be king, he will be happier, and his sons will be kings. Later, they predict Macbeth's doom. Macbeth gets very confused by their predictions.

Summary of the Main Characters in Shakespeare's *Macbeth*

Banquo, Leader in the King's *army*

He is a leader in Duncan's **army** along with Macbeth. He's also the subject of one of the **witches'** predictions. Unlike Macbeth, he does not act to fulfill these predictions. Instead, he relies on his better judgment and morals. After Macbeth arranges his murder, Banquo reappears as a ghost, which represents the guilt and anguish Macbeth is feeling over the murder.

Fleance

He is Banquo's son and the first in a line of kings as predicted by the Three **Witches**. He escapes when his father is killed. He represents a future Macbeth cannot bear: a line of kings following Banquo and not his own sons.

Macduff, *Thane* of Fife

He is a Scottish **nobleman** who begins to question Macbeth's unfair rule. Macbeth orders the murder of Macduff's wife and children. Macduff eventually joins Malcolm and the English forces to fight Macbeth and get **revenge** for the murder of his family. The **witches** tell Macbeth that he does not need to fear anyone "born of a woman," however Macduff was cut out of his mother's womb (Caesarian birth) meaning that he wasn't actually born of a woman. He is the man who kills Macbeth.

Siward, Earl of Northumberland

He is the leader of the English **army** and Duncan's brother. He leads an English **army** of ten thousand men against Macbeth. They disguise themselves with branches from Birnam Wood. He loses his son, Young Siward, to Macbeth.

Hecate, The "Queen" *Witch*

She demands loyalty and respect of the Three **Witches**. She makes fun of the Three **Witches** for helping an ungrateful Macbeth. She later commands them to tell Macbeth his future according to her will.

Link Map of Characters in Shakespeare's Macbeth

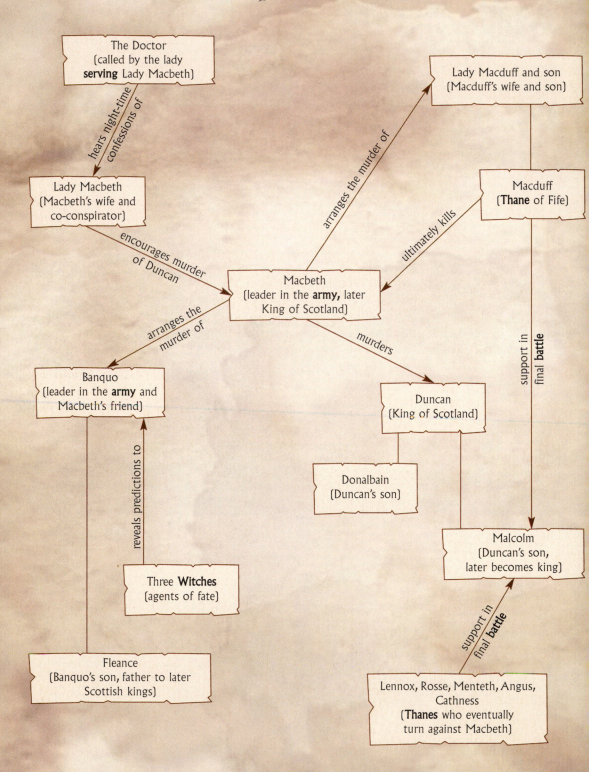

The Doctor
(called by the lady
serving Lady Macbeth)

Lady Macduff and son
(Macduff's wife and son)

*hears night-time
confessions of*

Lady Macbeth
(Macbeth's wife and
co-conspirator)

Macduff
(**Thane** of Fife)

arranges the murder of

ultimately kills

*encourages murder
of Duncan*

Macbeth
(leader in the **army,** later
King of Scotland)

*arranges the
murder of*

murders

*support in
final* **battle**

Banquo
(leader in the **army** and
Macbeth's friend)

Duncan
(King of Scotland)

reveals predictions to

Donalbain
(Duncan's son)

Three **Witches**
(agents of fate)

Malcolm
(Duncan's son,
later becomes king)

*support in
final* **battle**

Fleance
(Banquo's son, father to later
Scottish kings)

Lennox, Rosse, Menteth, Angus,
Cathness
(**Thanes** who eventually
turn against Macbeth)

Location	Shakespeare's Original	Adapted Text	Meaning
Act 1, Scene 1 Page 8	"When shall we three meet again? In thunder, lightning, or in rain? When the hurly-burly's done, When the battle's lost and won."	When shall we three meet again? In heavy storm or **pouring** rain? When one side's lost, and the other's won.	The three **witches** say this at the start of the play. They predict when they will meet with Macbeth and Banquo and tell each man of his future. Their meeting will begin the trouble that leads to the multiple murders of this play.
Act 1, Scene 1 Page 8	"Fair is foul, and foul is fair."	Fair is dark, and dark is fair.	The three **witches** say this at the beginning of the play. They tell about the coming events where good and **evil** will be turned upside down, when fair play will be destructive, and destruction will create fairness. Not long afterwards, Macbeth says in Act One, Scene Three that he has never seen such a foul and fair day before (both a good and bad day).
Act 1, Scene 3 Page 18	"If chance will have me King, why chance may crown me, Without my stir."	If I'm going to be king, it'll happen by itself.	Macbeth thinks this out loud after hearing the three **witches** predict that he will be made king. He thinks that he doesn't need to do anything but wait, and it will happen. In the end, however, this is what Banquo chooses to do, while Macbeth chooses to take it into his own hands and make it happen by murdering King Duncan.
Act 1, Scene 5 Page 20	"Yet do I fear thy nature: It is too full o'the milk of human-kindness."	But you're too kind to do what you have to do to become king.	Lady Macbeth says this as she reads a letter from her husband. In the letter, he tells her that the three **witches** predicted that he will be king. However, Lady Macbeth believes her husband is too weak, too kind, and too gentle to do what he must do to become king: murder Duncan.
Act 1, Scene 5 Page 22	"Look like the innocent flower, But be the serpent under't."	You mustn't let people know what you're planning. You must welcome him properly.	Lady Macbeth tells her husband to look sweet like a flower but to really be the snake (serpent) that is underneath the flower. She tells him that he should be very careful and to make sure nobody realizes that he is planning to become king by murder and lies.
Act 2, Scene 1 Page 31	"Is this a dagger which I see before me, The handle toward my hand?"	Is this a **dagger** I can see? Come here! Let me hold you!	Macbeth thinks he sees a **dagger** in front of him. He feels it is telling him to use it to stab his king. However he fears this **dagger** is not real but just something he imagines is there. As he is thinking all this, he uses a **dagger** to kill King Duncan.
Act 2, Scene 2 Page 36	"Will all great Neptune's ocean wash this blood Clean from my hand? No - this my hand will rather the multitudinous seas incarnadine, Making the green one red."	All the water in the ocean won't wash away this blood from my hands.	Macbeth says this to his wife after he has killed King Duncan. He feels terribly guilty and worries that the guilt will never disappear. His words are echoed later in Lady Macbeth's cries that she has blood on her hands.

Famous Quotations from Shakespeare's Macbeth

Location	Shakespeare's Original	Adapted Text	Meaning
Act 2, Scene 3 Page 45	"There's daggers in men's smiles."	Here there are knives in men's smiles.	Donalbain says this after realizing that his father, King Duncan, and his father's guards have been murdered. He and his brother, Malcolm, are suspicious and do not trust anyone, least of all the people who claim to be helping them get revenge for their father's death.
Act 4, Scene 1 Page 78	"Double, double toil and trouble; Fire burn, and cauldron bubble."	Double, double toil and trouble, fire, burn and make it bubble.	The three **witches** chant this spell as they dance around the potion they are cooking on the fire. They want to double the amount of trouble about to happen. Their words increase the audience's anticipation that the action is about reach a high point.
Act 5, Scene 1 Page 105	"Out, damned spot! Out, I say!"	Out! Out, I say!	Lady Macbeth cries this as she desperately tries to clean her hands. She is sleepwalking and believes her hands are covered in blood. Her guilt causes her to see the blood. The doctor and servant who are watching tell the reader that Lady Macbeth's hands are clean already.
Act 5, Scene 1 Page 106	" … all the perfumes of Arabia will not sweeten this little hand."	I can still smell the blood. Nothing will make my little hand smell sweet again.	Lady Macbeth continues to talk as she sleepwalks. She says again and again that her hands are stained with blood and truly believes, in her sleep, that she will never be able to wash her hands of their dirty, guilty secret.
Act 5, Scene 5 Page 118	"Out, out, brief candle! Life's but a walking shadow, a poor player That struts and frets his hour upon the stage, And then is heard no more. It is a tale told by an idiot, full of sound and fury, signifying nothing."	Life is just a walking shadow. It's a story that a fool tells — full of noise but with no meaning.	Macbeth says this in sadness and despair when he learns that his wife, the Queen, is dead. He realizes that life is short and often finished before it even begins. It is a bleak and remorseful view, for he now thinks that while life appears to contain much promise, it is actually empty and meaningless.

Notes

Notes

Notes

OTHER CLASSICAL COMICS TITLES:

Henry V

Published August 2008

Frankenstein

Published Fall 2008

Great Expectations

Published Fall 2008

Jane Eyre

Published Early 2009